CONTENTS

Words that look like **this** can be found in the glossary on page 24.

KU-587-108

WHAT IS CULTURE?

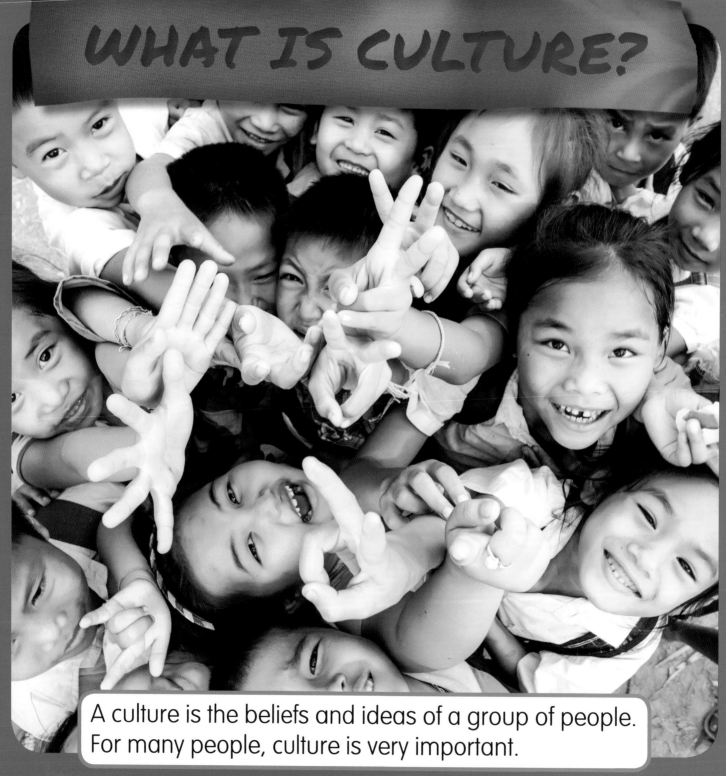

A culture is the beliefs and ideas of a group of people. For many people, culture is very important.

Many things go into making a culture.

Food

History

Traditions

Religion

Location

Communities

WHAT MAKES A CULTURE?

Art

Clothes

Family

5

WHERE IS CHINA?

Mongolia

China

Nepal

China is a country in Asia. It borders lots of other countries, including Mongolia to the north and Nepal to the southwest.

China is one of the biggest countries in the world. The **population** of China is over 1.3 billion.

Beijing is China's **capital city**.

LANGUAGES

Most people in China speak Mandarin. Mandarin is the most spoken language in the world.

People in China use a different **writing system** to English. Instead of using letters to create words, they write using symbols that can stand for whole words.

你 好

nǐ hǎo

This means 'Hello!' in Mandarin.

FOOD

Chopsticks

Food is a big part of Chinese culture. Traditionally, meals have two parts: the fàn, which is the rice or noodles, and the tsai, which is the meat and vegetables.

People in China use chopsticks to eat rather than knives and forks. Spoons are used to eat Chinese soups and stews, such as congee.

Congee

SPORT

Martial arts are very popular in China. Martial arts are fighting techniques that were used by soldiers throughout China's history.

The 2008 Olympic Games were held in China. China won more gold medals than any other country.

The Olympic stadium in Beijing is known as the Bird's Nest.

CLOTHING

In the past, rich people in China wore clothes made of silk. The people of China were the first to make silk.

A **formal** piece of clothing worn by women in China is the cheongsam. A cheongsam is a silk dress with a high collar.

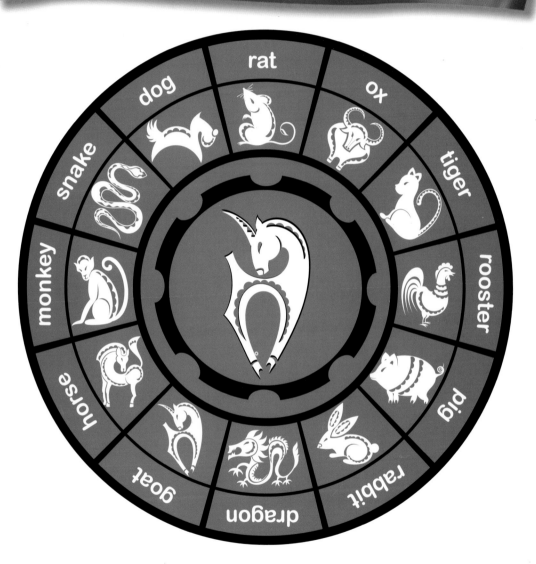

One of the most important parts of Chinese culture is the celebration of Chinese New Year. Every new year is linked to an animal.

Chinese New Year celebrates the story of how Nian was defeated by the Chinese people. Nian was a giant beast who was said to live in the mountains in China.

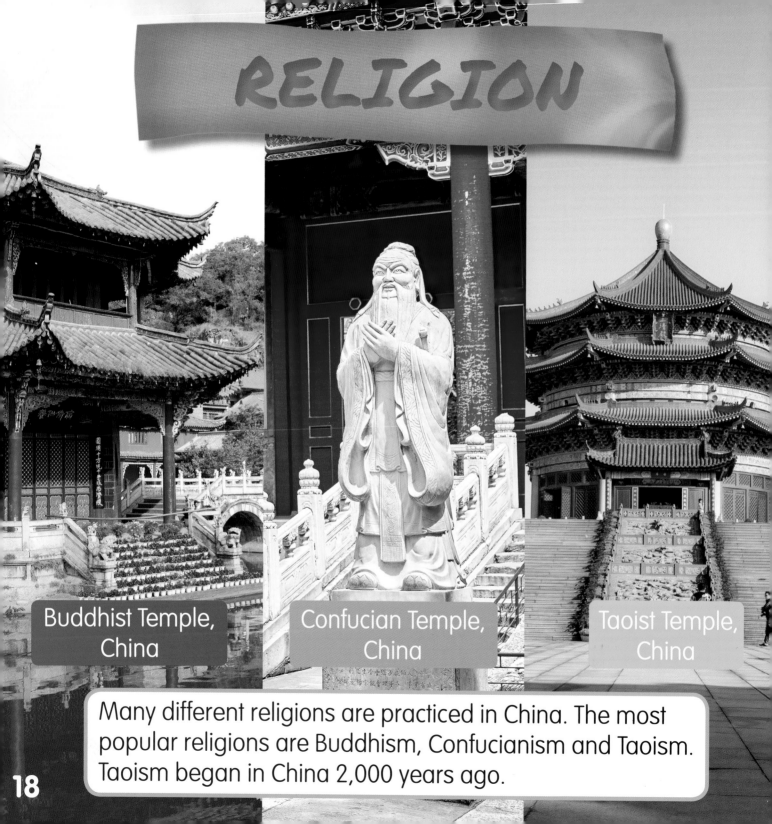

RELIGION

Buddhist Temple, China

Confucian Temple, China

Taoist Temple, China

Many different religions are practiced in China. The most popular religions are Buddhism, Confucianism and Taoism. Taoism began in China 2,000 years ago.

Buddhism has had a big effect on art in China. The Mogao Caves in China are home to thousands of Buddhist statues.

Art is very important in Chinese culture. Painting, poetry and calligraphy were traditionally known as 'the three perfections'. Calligraphy is the art of handwriting.

China is known for its blue and white pottery. This way of painting pottery began in China around 700 years ago and has become a traditional style of Chinese art.

Vase

LANDMARKS

The Great Wall of China is over 21,000 kilometres long.

Landmarks can tell us a lot about a country's history and culture. The Great Wall of China is a famous Chinese landmark. It was built to keep out invaders from the north.

Lots of people see the Great Wall of China as a symbol of Chinese history and culture. Over 10 million **tourists** go to see the Great Wall of China every year.

GLOSSARY

capital city	the city where a country's laws are made
formal	traditional and suitable for important events
landmarks	places or buildings that are famous or easily recognised
population	the number of people living in a place
tourists	people who are visiting a place for pleasure
writing system	the method used to write a language

INDEX

Series editor: Philip Prowse

The Sugar Glider

Rod Neilsen

CAMBRIDGE
UNIVERSITY PRESS

CAMBRIDGE UNIVERSITY PRESS
Cambridge, New York, Melbourne, Madrid, Cape Town, Singapore, São Paulo

Cambridge University Press
The Edinburgh Building, Cambridge CB2 2RU, UK

www.cambridge.org
Information on this title: www.cambridge.org/9780521536615

First published 2003
7th printing 2006

Printed in the United Kingdom at the University Press, Cambridge

A catalogue record for this publication is available from the British Library

ISBN-13 978-0-521-53661-5 paperback
ISBN-10 0-521-53661-8 paperback

ISBN-13 978-0-521-68651-8 paperback plus audio CD pack
ISBN-10 0-521-68651-2 paperback plus audio CD pack